CW01375820

Catch Them If You Can

Selected by
Helen Cook and
Morag Styles

Illustrated by
Jane Gedye
Errol Lloyd and
Penelope Taylor

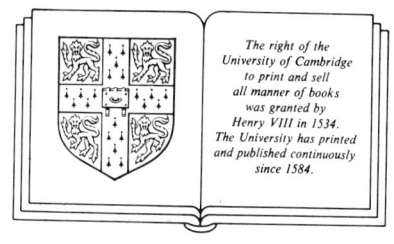

The right of the
University of Cambridge
to print and sell
all manner of books
was granted by
Henry VIII in 1534.
The University has printed
and published continuously
since 1584.

Cambridge University Press

Cambridge
New York   Port Chester
Melbourne   Sydney

Published by the Press Syndicate of the University of Cambridge
The Pitt Building, Trumpington Street, Cambridge CB2 1RP
40 West 20th Street, New York, NY 10011-4211, USA
10 Stamford Road, Oakleigh, Melbourne 3166, Australia

© Cambridge University Press 1991

First published 1991

Printed in Great Britain at the University Press, Cambridge

British Library cataloguing in publication data
Catch Them If You Can.
1. Poetry in English – Anthologies
I. Cook, Helen 1954–   II. Styles, Morag
821.008

ISBN 0 521 39058 3

Contents

Bananas in Pyjamas

Carey Blyton	Bananas in Pyjamas 9
Gina Wilson	Jim-Jam Pyjamas 10
Spike Milligan	Ode to the Queen on her Jubilee 11
Anon	Humpty Dumpty 12
Michael Rosen	Humpty Dumpty 12
Anon	Piggy on the Railway 13
From *Jamaica Maddah Goose*	Dis Lickle Pig 14
Michael Rosen	This Little Pig 15
Anon	The Man in the Wilderness 16
Edward Lear	There was an Old Man in a Tree 17
Lewis Carroll	Twinkle, Twinkle, Little Bat! 18
William Cole	Back Yard, July Night 19
Jane Taylor	EXTRACT FROM The Star 19
Terry Jones	Pet Food 20
Adrian Mitchell	Nature Poem 22
Anon	The Squirrel 23
Eloise Greenfield	Rope Rhyme 24
Anon	Jumping Joan 26
Traditional, Nigeria	The One who does not Love Me 27
Libby Houston	Black Dot 28
Anon	The Frog 29
Roger McGough	P's and Q's 30
Roger McGough	To Amuse Emus 30
Harry Graham	Ruthless Rhyme Five 31
Colin McNaughton	Short Sharp Shock 31
Dennis Lee	The Gentle Giant 32
Michael Rosen	Have You Seen the Hidebehind? 34
Jane Yolen	Dragon Night 35
Ogden Nash	Sweet Dreams 36

Don't Do That

Spike Milligan	Kids 41
Michael Rosen	Don't 42
Karla Kuskin	I Woke Up This Morning 44
Jack Prelutsky	Suzanna Socked Me Sunday 46
Emma Reid (aged 9)	Bossy Parrot (My Sister) 47
Nikki Giovanni	Parents Never Understand 48
Colin McNaughton	Monday's Child is Red and Spotty 49
John Agard	A-So It Go 50
Anon	A Rhyme for a Nosey Parker 51
Anon	Policeman, Policeman 52
Kit Wright	Dave Dirt Came to Dinner 53
Errol Lloyd	Blame the Parents 54
Judith Nicholls	Teacher Said . . . 55
Wendy Cope	Twiddling Your Thumbs 56
Rebecca Halliday (aged 8)	Never 58
Anon	Burp 59
Playground rhyme	Mother Made a Seedy Cake 59
John Agard	Don't Call Alligator Long-Mouth Till You Cross River 60
Charles Causley	Good Morning, Mr Croco-doco-dile 61
A A Milne	Come Out with Me 62
David McCord	Father and I in the Woods 63
Seamus Heaney	EXTRACT FROM Clearances 64
Brian Patten	Rules 66
Lewis Carrol	Speak Roughly to Your Little Boy 68

Pussy Cat, Pussy Cat

Traditional	Pussy Cat, Pussy Cat 73
Spike Milligan	Pussy Cat, Pussy Cat 73
Edwin Thumboo	Fluffy 74
Ian (aged 7)	Who am I? 75
Karla Kuskin	If You . . . 76
Keith Bosley	Cat 77
William Carlos Williams	Poem 78
e e cummings	Why Did You Go? 79
Eleanor Farjeon	A Kitten 80
Valerie Worth	Cat 82
Traditional, Gaelic	The Cat 83
Elizabeth Coatsworth	On a Night of Snow 84
Mick Gowar	EXTRACT FROM Hunting with Henry the Cat 86
Kit Wright	Granny Tom 88
Ann Bonner	Fat Cat 89
Roger McGough	Bring Back the Cat 90
Stevie Smith	The Singing Cat 92
Mervyn Peake	Uncle Paul of Pimlico 94
Vita Sackville-West	The Greater Cats 95
Valerie Worth	Tiger 96
W J Turner	EXTRACT FROM India 97
Chinese proverb	There are Times 97
Karla Kuskin	Roar 98
Sarah Harris (aged 8)	Tiger, Tiger 99
William Blake	EXTRACT FROM The Tyger 100

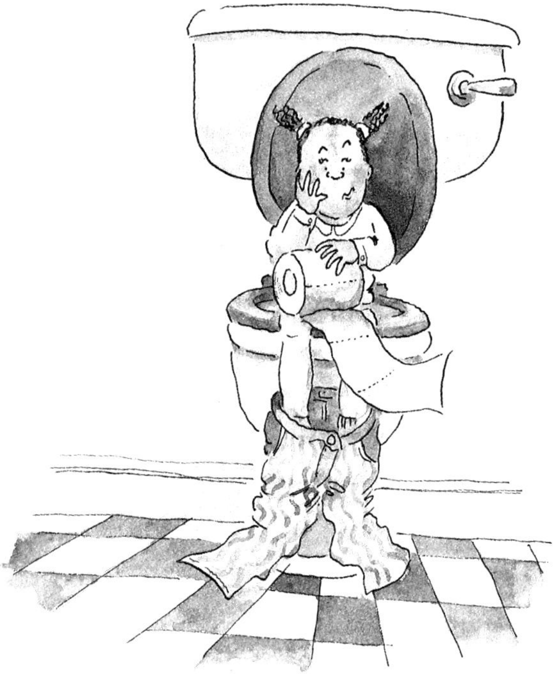

Bananas in Pyjamas

Bananas in Pyjamas

Bananas,
In pyjamas,
Are coming down the stairs;
Bananas,
In pyjamas,
Are coming down in pairs;
Bananas,
In pyjamas,
Are chasing teddy bears –
'Cos on Tuesdays
They all try to
CATCH THEM UNAWARES.

Carey Blyton

Jim-Jam Pyjamas

He wears striped jim-jam pyjamas,
You never saw jim-jams like those –
A fine-fitting, stretchy, fur cat-suit,
Skin-tight from his head to his toes.

He wears striped jim-jam pyjamas,
Black and yellow and dashingly gay;
He makes certain that everyone sees them
By keeping them on all the day.

He wears striped jim-jam pyjamas,
He walks with a smug-pussy stride;
There's no hiding his pride in his jim-jams
With their zig-zaggy lines down each side.

He wears striped jim-jam pyjamas
And pauses at times to display
The effect as he flexes his torso –
Then he fancies he hears people say:

'I wish I had jim-jam pyjamas!
I wish I were feline and slim!
Oh, look at that brave Bengal tiger!
Oh, how I should love to be him!'

Gina Wilson

Ode to the Queen on Her Jubilee

Sound the trumpet,
Bang the drum,
Shake the tambourine
Because this year is Jubilee
But only for the Quine.
So glory, glory,
Gloria!
Regina gloriana!
You are the apple
Of my eye
Let me be your banana!

Spike Milligan

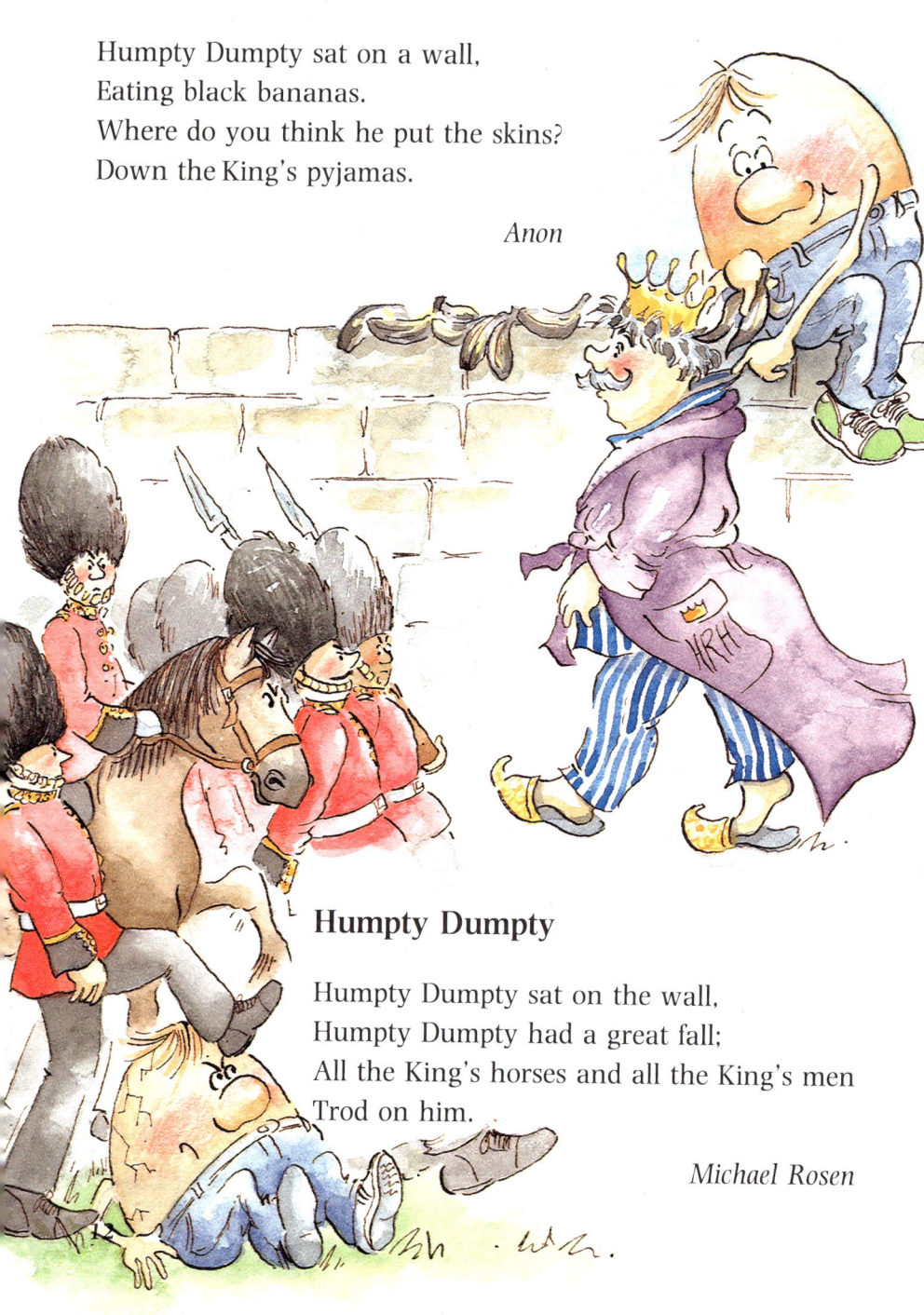

Humpty Dumpty

Humpty Dumpty sat on a wall,
Eating black bananas.
Where do you think he put the skins?
Down the King's pyjamas.

Anon

Humpty Dumpty

Humpty Dumpty sat on the wall,
Humpty Dumpty had a great fall;
All the King's horses and all the King's men
Trod on him.

Michael Rosen

Piggy on the Railway

Piggy on the railway
Picking up stones,
Along came an engine
And broke Piggy's bones.

'Oy,' said Piggy,
'That's not fair.'
'Pooh,' said the engine driver,
'I don't care.'

Anon

Dis Lickle Pig

Dis lickle pig go a markit,
   Dis lickle pig tan a yaad,
Dis lickle pig nyam curry goat,
   Dis lickle pig got nun,
Dis lickle pig holla, 'Wahi, wahi, wahi!'
   All de way a im yaad.

From *Jamaica Maddah Goose*

This Little Pig

This little pig went to market,
This little pig ate some ants,
This little pig went to Sainsbury's,
This little pig went up in a lift,
And this little pig
Went wee wee wee wee wee wee,
Oh no, I've wet my pants.

Michael Rosen

The Man in the Wilderness

The man in the wilderness asked of me,
How many strawberries grow in the sea?
I answered him as I thought good
As many red herrings as grow in a wood.

Anon

There was an Old Man in a Tree

There was an old man in a tree,
Whose whiskers were lovely to see;
But the birds of the air pluck'd them perfectly bare,
To make themselves nests in that tree.

Edward Lear

Twinkle, Twinkle, Little Bat!

Twinkle, twinkle, little bat!
How I wonder what you're at!
Up above the world you fly,
Like a tea-tray in the sky.

Lewis Carroll

Back Yard, July Night

Firefly, airplane, satellite, star –
How I wonder which you are.

William Cole

EXTRACT FROM **The Star**

As your bright and tiny spark
Lights the traveller in the dark,
Though I know not what you are,
Twinkle, twinkle, little star.

Jane Taylor

Pet Food

What do you get, Jude,
When you eat Pet Food?

Hamsterburgers,
Poodle Pies,
Goldfish Fingers,
Canary Fries.

Budgie Bangers,
Dachshunds and Mash,
Pickled Parrots,
Corned Cat Hash.

Gerbils on Toast,
Tortoise Teas,
Horse-in-a-basket,
Mice and Peas.

That's what you get, Jude,
When you eat Pet Food!

Terry Jones

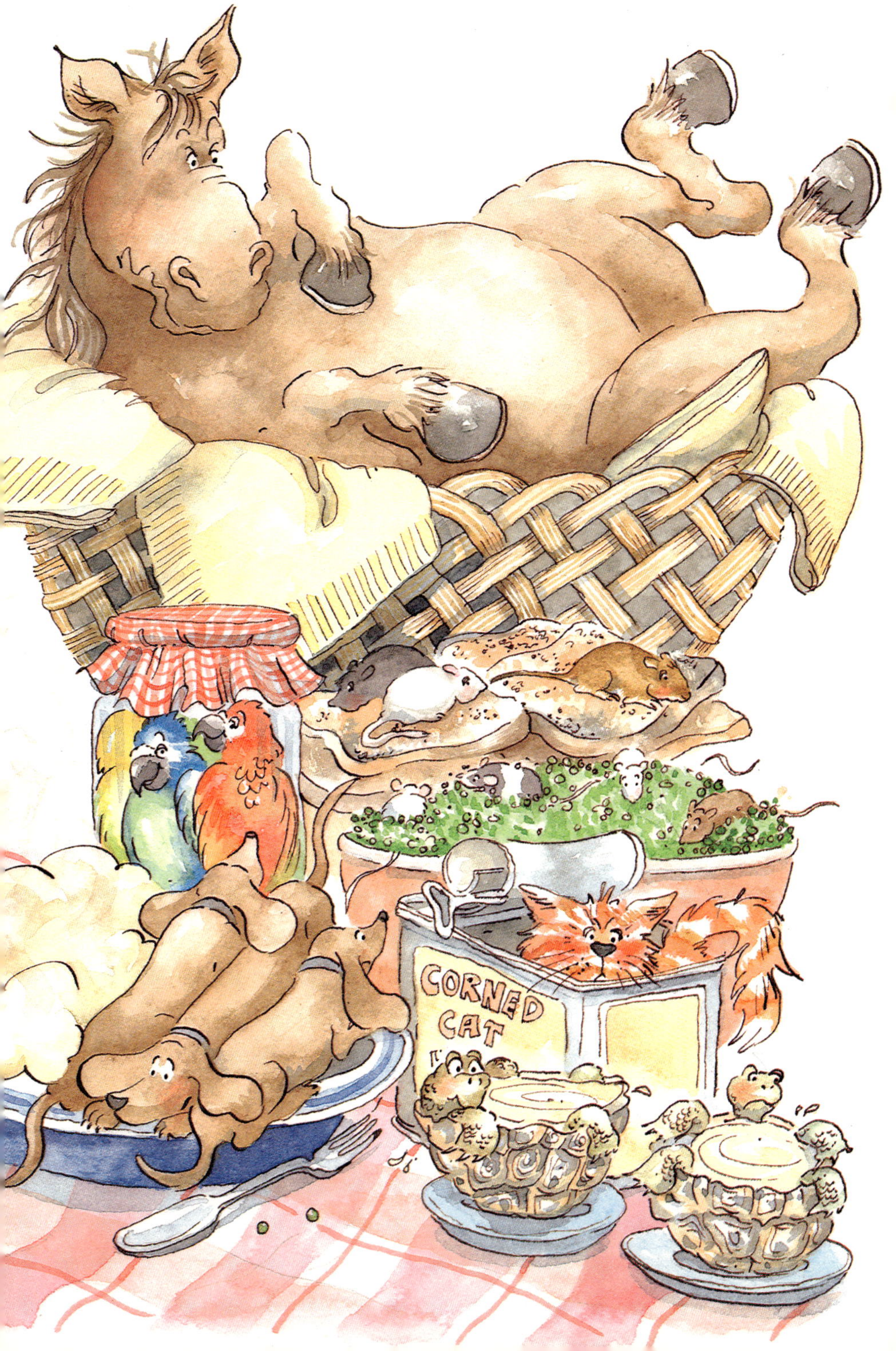
CORNED CAT

Nature Poem

Skylark, what prompts your silver song
To fountain up and down the sky?

>   Beetles roast
>   With fleas on toast
>   And earthworm pie.

Adrian Mitchell

The Squirrel

The winds they did blow,
The leaves they did wag;
Along came a beggar boy
And put me in a bag.

He took me to London,
A lady did me buy,
Put me in a silver cage
And hung me up on high.

With apples by the fire
And nuts for to crack,
Besides a little feather bed
To rest my little back.

Anon

Rope Rhyme

Get set, ready now, jump right in
Bounce and kick and giggle and spin
Listen to the rope when it hits the ground
Listen to that clappedy-slappedy sound
Jump right up when it tells you to
Come back down whatever you do
Count to a hundred, count by ten
Start to count all over again

                    That's what jumping is all about
                    Get set, ready now,

jump

right

out!

Eloise Greenfield

Jumping Joan

Here am I,

Little Jumping Joan;

When nobody's with me

I'm all alone.

Anon

The One who does not Love Me

The one who does not love me,
He will become a frog
And he will jump jump jump away:
He will become a monkey with one leg
And he will hop hop hop away.

Traditional, Nigeria

Black Dot

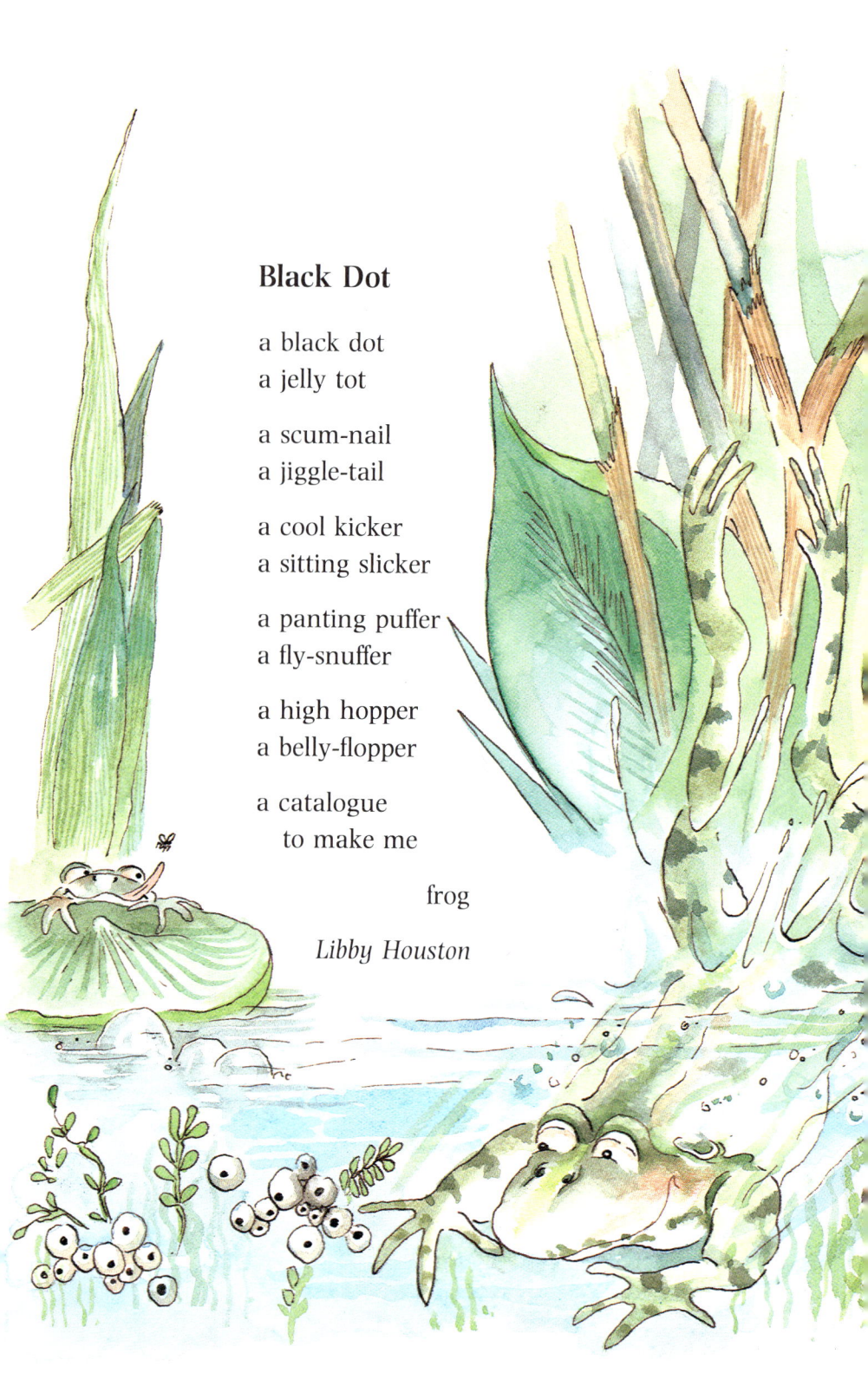

a black dot
a jelly tot

a scum-nail
a jiggle-tail

a cool kicker
a sitting slicker

a panting puffer
a fly-snuffer

a high hopper
a belly-flopper

a catalogue
 to make me

              frog

Libby Houston

The Frog

What a wonderful bird the frog are –
When he sit, he stand almost;
When he hop, he fly almost.
He ain't got no sense hardly;
He ain't got no tail hardly either.
When he sit, he sit on what he ain't got – almost.

Anon

P's and Q's

I quite often confuse
My quees and my poos.

> Roger McGough

To Amuse Emus

To amuse
   emus
on warm summer nights

   Kiwis
do wiwis
from spectacular heights.

> Roger McGough

Ruthless Rhyme Five

Father heard his children scream,
So he threw them in the stream,
Saying, as he dropped the third,
'Children should be seen not heard.'

Harry Graham

Short Sharp Shock

If your children are ever unruly,
(Of course this might never happen),
Just tell them to kindly behave themselves,
Then reach over quickly and slap 'em!

Colin McNaughton

The Gentle Giant

Every night
At twelve o'clock,
The gentle giant
Takes a walk;
With a cry cried high
And a call called low,
The gentle giant
Walks below.

And as he walks,
He cries, he calls:

'Bad men, boogie men,
Bully men, shoo!
No one in the neighbourhood
Is scared of you.
The children are asleep,
And the parents are too:
Bad men, boogie men,
Bully men, shoo!'

Dennis Lee

Have You Seen the Hidebehind?

Have you seen the Hidebehind?
I don't think you will, mind you,
because as you're running through the dark
the Hidebehind's behind you.

Michael Rosen

Dragon Night

Little flame mouths,
Cool your tongues.
Dreamtime starts,
My furnace lungs.

Rest your wings now,
Little flappers,
Cave mouth calls
To dragon nappers.

Night is coming,
Bank your fire.
Time for dragons
To retire.

Hiss.
Hush.
Sleep.

Jane Yolen

Sweet Dreams

I wonder as into bed I creep
What it feels like to fall asleep.
I've told myself stories, I've counted sheep,
But I'm always asleep when I fall asleep.
Tonight my eyes I will open keep,
And I'll stay awake till I fall asleep,
Then I'll know what it feels like to fall asleep,
Asleep,
Asleeep,
Asleeeep . . .

Ogden Nash

Don't Do That!

Kids

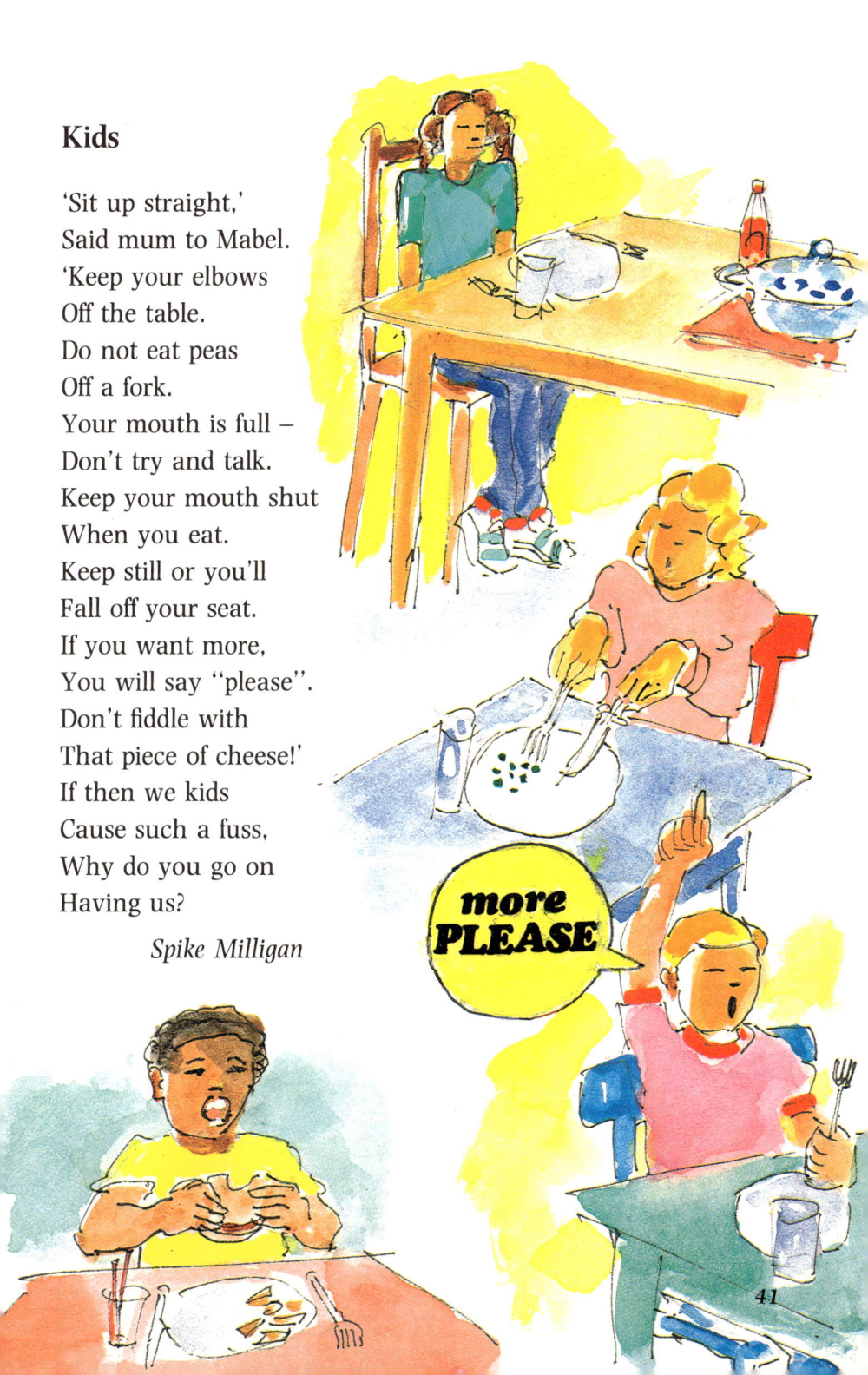

'Sit up straight,'
Said mum to Mabel.
'Keep your elbows
Off the table.
Do not eat peas
Off a fork.
Your mouth is full –
Don't try and talk.
Keep your mouth shut
When you eat.
Keep still or you'll
Fall off your seat.
If you want more,
You will say "please".
Don't fiddle with
That piece of cheese!'
If then we kids
Cause such a fuss,
Why do you go on
Having us?

Spike Milligan

Don't

Don't do,
Don't do,
Don't do that.
Don't pull faces,
Don't tease the cat.

Don't pick your ears,
Don't be rude at school.
Who do they think I am?

Some kind of fool?

One day
they'll say
Don't put toffee in my coffee
don't pour gravy on the baby
don't put beer in his ear
don't stick your toes up his nose.

Don't put confetti on the spaghetti
and don't squash peas on your knees.

Don't put ants in your pants
don't put mustard in the custard

don't chuck jelly at the telly

and don't throw fruit at the computer
don't throw fruit at the computer.

Don't what?
Don't throw fruit at the computer.
Don't what?
Don't throw fruit at the computer.
Who do they think I am?
Some kind of fool?

Michael Rosen

I Woke Up This Morning

I woke up this morning
At quarter past seven.
I kicked up the covers
And stuck out my toe.
And ever since then
(That's a quarter past seven)
They haven't said anything
Other than 'no'.

They haven't said anything
Other than 'Please, dear,
Don't do what you're doing,'
Or 'Lower your voice.'
And however I've chosen,
I've done the wrong thing
And I've made the wrong choice.

I didn't wash well
And I didn't say thank you.
I didn't shake hands
And I didn't say please.
I didn't say sorry
When, passing the candy,
I banged the box into
Miss Witelson's knees.
I didn't say sorry.
I didn't stand straighter.
I didn't speak louder
When asked what I'd said.

Well, I said
That tomorrow
At quarter past seven,
They can
Come in and get me
I'M STAYING IN BED.

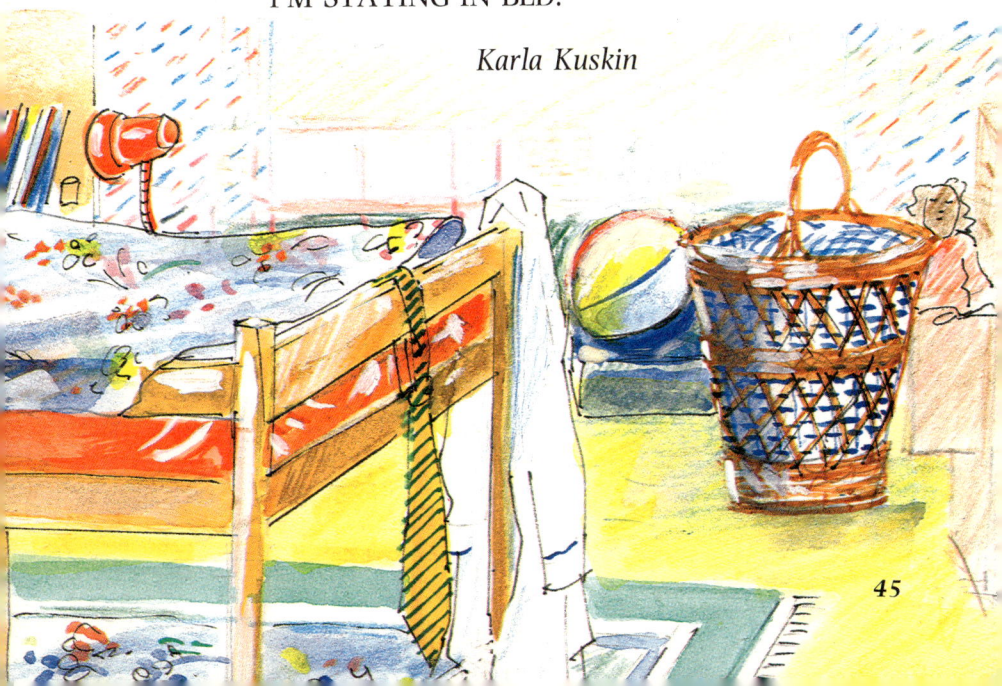

Karla Kuskin

Suzanna Socked Me Sunday

Suzanna socked me Sunday,
she socked me Monday, too,
she also socked me Tuesday,
I was turning black and blue.

She socked me double Wednesday,
and Thursday even more,
but when she socked me Friday,
she began to get me sore.

'Enough's enough,' I yelled at her,
'I hate it when you hit me!'
'Well, then I won't!' Suzanna said –
that Saturday, she bit me.

Jack Prelutsky

Bossy Parrot (My Sister)

Mum said, PIANO! Emma,
   Bossy Parrot said, Mum said piano!

Mum said, BATH! Emma,
   Bossy Parrot said, Mum said bath!

Mum said, SUPPER! Emma,
   Bossy Parrot said, Mum said supper!

That does it, I said.
Homework!! Move your blazer!
Move your bag!
My sister is a Bossy Parrot!!!

Emma Reid (aged 9)

Parents Never Understand

well i can't 'cause
yesterday when mommy had
this important visitor she said
run along joey and let mommy talk
and i ran along upstairs to see
bobby and eddie and we were playing
and forgot and i had to come down
stairs and get dry clothes and mommy said how
could an eight year old boy wet his pants
and i looked at the visitor and smiled a really nice
smile and said i guess in america anything
can happen
so mommy said i have to
stay in today

Nikki Giovanni

Monday's Child is Red and Spotty

Monday's child is red and spotty,
Tuesday's child won't use the potty.
Wednesday's child won't go to bed,
Thursday's child will not be fed.
Friday's child breaks all his toys,
Saturday's child makes an awful noise.
And the child that's born on the seventh day
Is a pain in the neck like the rest, OK!

Colin McNaughton

A-So It Go

So mouthy-mouthy
so mouthy-mouthy
you got so much
MOUTHABILITY!
A-so it go
A-so it go
when yuh mouth can't stop flow

So wanty-wanty
so wanty-wanty
you got so much
WANTABILITY!
A-so it go
A-so it go
when you wanty dis and wanty dat

So laughy-laughy
so laughy-laughy
you got so much
LAUGHABILITY!
Take care one day you laughy-laughy
till you burst
yuh belly-belly

John Agard

A Rhyme for a Nosey Parker

Ask no questions
And you'll be told no lies;
Shut your mouth
And you'll catch no flies.

Anon

Policeman, Policeman

Policeman, policeman
  don't catch me!
Catch that boy
  behind that tree.
He stole apples,
  I stole none;
Put him in the jailhouse,
  just for fun.

Anon

Dave Dirt Came to Dinner

Dave Dirt came to dinner
   And he stuck his chewing gum
Underneath the table
   And it didn't please my Mum

And it didn't please my Granny
   Who was quite a sight to see
When she got up from the table
   With the gum stuck to her knee

Where she put her cup and saucer
   When she sat and drank her tea
And the saucer and the chewing gum
   Got stuck as stuck can be

And she staggered round the kitchen
   With a saucer on her skirt –
No, it didn't please my Granny
   But it
      PLEASED
      DAVE
        DIRT

              Kit Wright

Blame the Parents

I blame the parents
said Miss,
I really do.
They just don't know how to say no.
They don't know how to say no
to TV
They don't know how to say no
to videos
They don't know how to say no
to bike riding
They don't know how to say no
to playing outside
They don't know how to say no
to ice-cream
They don't know how to say no
to karate.
I wouldn't
send my child to karate.
Would you?

Errol Lloyd

Teacher Said . . .

You can use
   mumbled and muttered,
   groaned, grumbled and uttered,
   professed, droned or stuttered
         . . . but *don't* use SAID!

You can use
   rant or recite,
   yell, yodel or snort,
   bellow, murmur or moan,
   you can grunt or just groan
         . . . but *don't* use SAID!

You can
   hum, howl and hail,
   scream, screech, shriek or bawl,
   squeak, snivel or squeal
   with a blood-curdling wail
         . . . but *don't* use SAID!

         . . . SAID my teacher.

Judith Nicholls

Twiddling Your Thumbs

When you've finished all your writing
And you've got stuck with your sums
And you need to see your teacher
But your turn never comes,
You may have time to practise this –
Twiddling your thumbs.

Round and round and round they go,
Forwards, backwards, fast or slow,
Then, if you should get the chance,
Make them do a little dance.

When you've eaten up your dinner,
Including all the crumbs,
And you're waiting for permission
To go out with your chums,
Here's a way to pass the time –
Twiddling your thumbs.

Round and round and round they go,
Forwards, backwards, fast or slow,
Then, if you should get the chance,
Make them do a little dance.

If you have to go out visiting
With aunts and dads and mums
And its boring being with grown-ups
All sitting on their bums,
Don't scream and bite the carpet –
Try twiddling your thumbs.

Round and round and round they go,
Forwards, backwards, fast or slow,
Then, if you should get the chance,
Make them do a little dance.

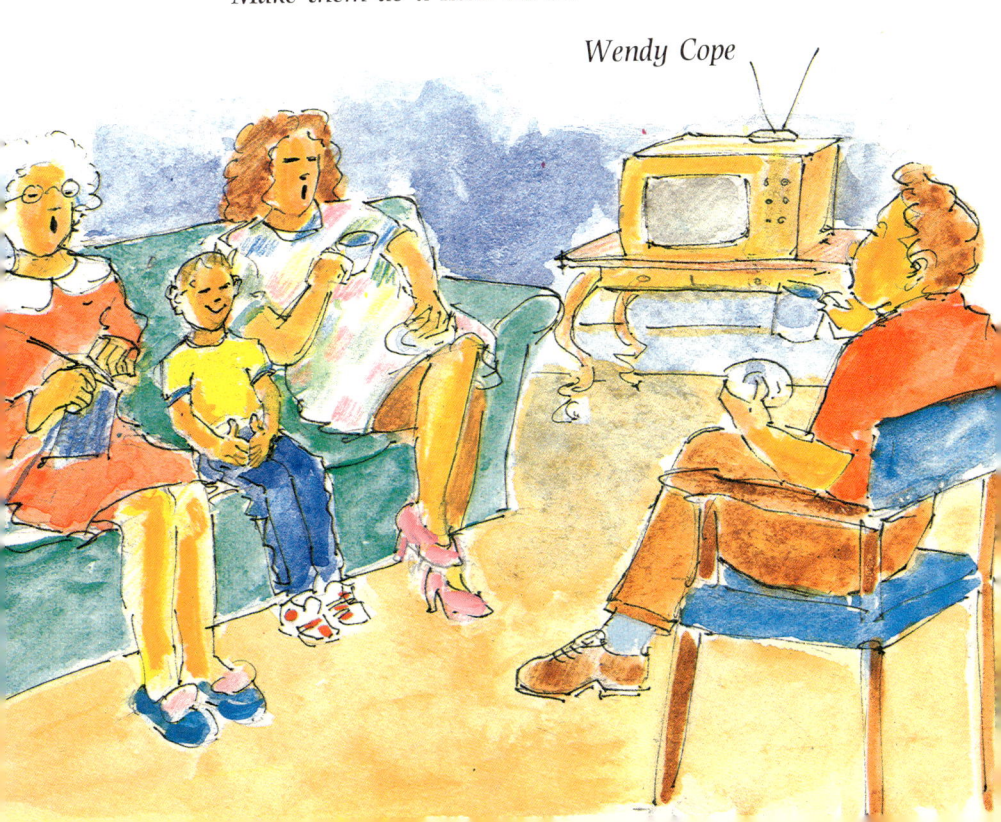

Wendy Cope

Never

Mummy says never run on the road.
Daddy says never cheat.
My brother says never play with his toys.
Nanny says never kiss the boys.
Grandad says never a secret tell.
I'm sick, sore and tired of being told,
    Never!

Rebecca Halliday (aged 8)

Burp

Pardon me
for being so rude.
It was not me
It was my food.
It just came up
to say hallo.
Now it's gone
back down below.

Anon

Mother Made a Seedy Cake

Mother made a seedy cake,
Gave us all the belly ache;
Father bought a pint of beer,
Gave us all the diarrhoea.

Playground rhyme

Don't Call Alligator Long-Mouth Till You Cross River

Call alligator long-mouth
call alligator saw-mouth
call alligator pushy-mouth
call alligator scissors-mouth
call alligator raggedy-mouth
call alligator bumpy-bum
call alligator all dem rude word
but better wait
           till you cross river.

John Agard

Good Morning, Mr Croco-doco-dile

Good morning, Mr Croco-doco-dile,
And how are you today?
I like to see you croco-smoco-smile
In your croco-woco-way.

From the tip of your beautiful croco-toco-tail
To your croco-hoco-head
You seem to me so croco-stoco-still
As if you're croco-doco-dead.

Perhaps if I touch your croco-cloco-claw
Or your croco-snoco-snout,
Or get up close to your croco-joco-jaw
I shall very soon find out.

But suddenly I croco-soco-see
In your croco-oco-eye
A curious kind of croco-gloco-gleam,
So I just don't think I'll try.

Forgive me, Mr Croco-doco-dile
But it's time I was away.
Let's talk a little croco-woco-while
Another croco-doco-day.

Charles Causley

Come Out with Me

There's sun on the river and sun on the hill . . .
You can hear the sea if you stand quite still!
There's eight new puppies at Roundabout Farm –
And I saw an old sailor with only one arm!

    But every one says, 'Run along!'
        (Run along, run along!)
   All of them say 'Run along! I'm busy as can be.'
      Every one says, 'Run along,
       There's a little darling!'
If I'm a little darling, why don't they run with me?

There's wind on the river and wind on the hill . . .
There's a dark dead water-wheel under the mill!
I saw a fly which had just been drowned –
And I know where a rabbit goes into the ground!

    But every one says, 'Run along!'
        (Run along, run along!)
   All of them say 'Yes, dear,' and never notice me.
      Every one says, 'Run along,
       There's a little darling!'
If I'm a little darling, why won't they come and see?

A A Milne

Father and I in the Woods

'Son,'
My father used to say,
'Don't run.'

'Walk,'
My father used to say,
'Don't talk.'

'Words,'
My father used to say,
'Scare birds.'

So be:
It's sky and brook and bird
And tree.

David McCord

EXTRACT FROM **Clearances**

Polished linoleum shone there. Brass taps shone.
The china cups were very white and big –
An unchipped set with sugar bowl and jug.
The kettle whistled. Sandwich and teascone
Were present and correct. In case it run,
The butter must be kept out of the sun.
And don't be dropping crumbs. Don't tilt your chair.
Don't reach. Don't point. Don't make noise when you stir.

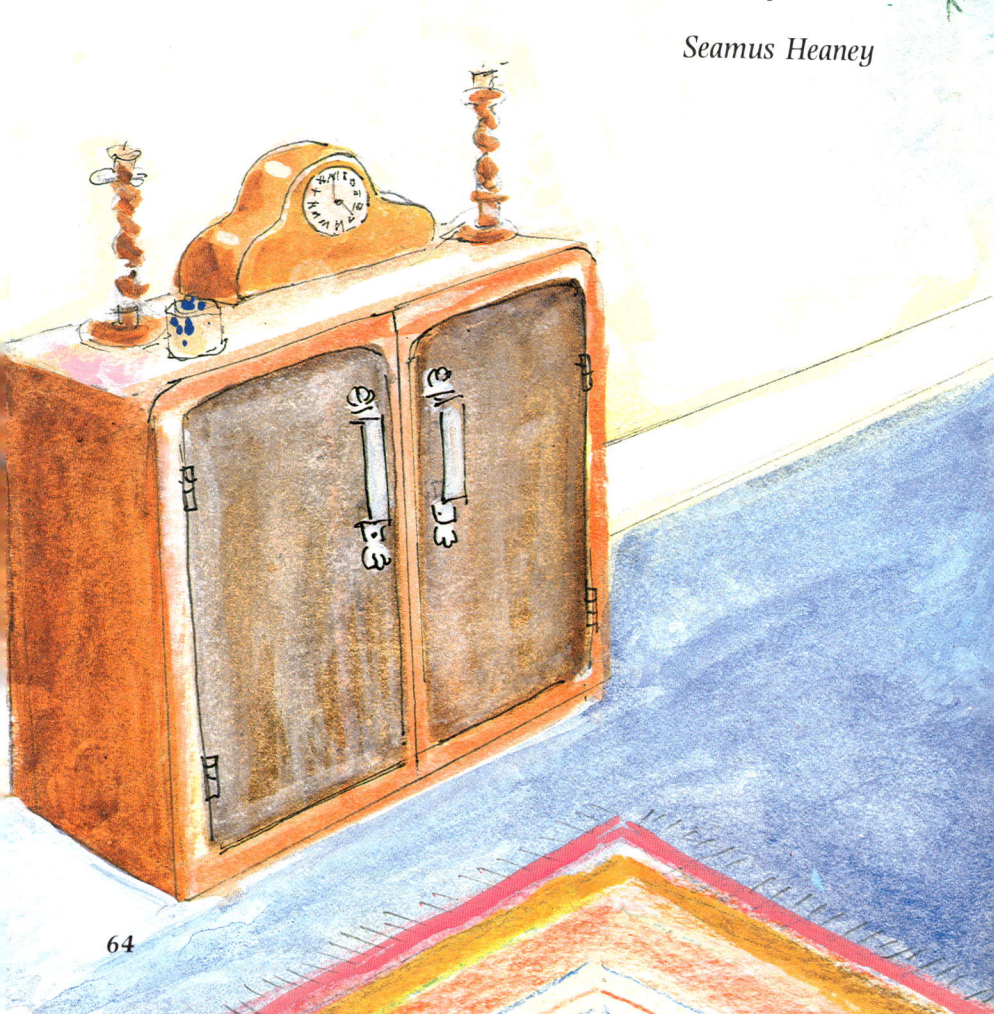

Seamus Heaney

65

Rules

Governments rule most countries,
Bankers rule most banks,
Captains rule their football teams
And piranhas rule fish tanks.

There are rules for gnobling gnomes
And rules for frying frogs,
There are rules for biting bullies
And for vexing vicious dogs.

There are rules for driving motor cars
And crashing into chums,
There are rules for taking off your pants
And showing spotty bums.

There are rules for nasty children
Who tie bangers to old cats,
There are rules for running riot
And rules for burning bats.

There are rules in the classroom.
There are rules in the street.
Some rules are wild and woolly
And some are tame and neat.

And some are pretty sensible
And some are pretty daft;
Some I take quite seriously,
At others I have laughed,

But there is one special rule
You should not be without:
If you do not like the rules
OPEN YOUR MOUTH AND SHOUT!
OPEN YOUR MOUTH AND SHOUT!

Brian Patten

Speak Roughly to Your Little Boy

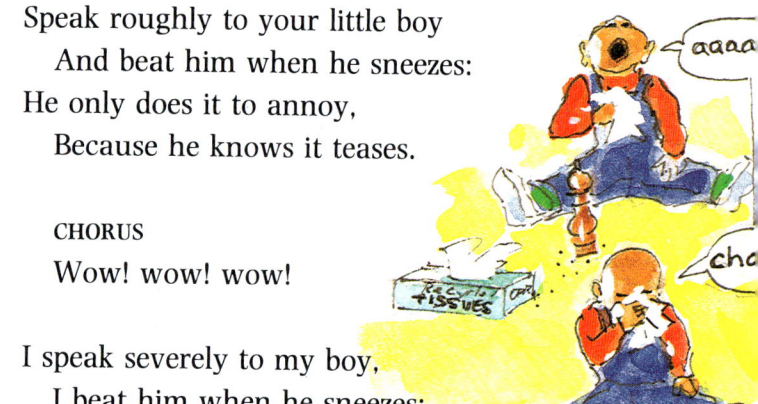

Speak roughly to your little boy
   And beat him when he sneezes:
He only does it to annoy,
   Because he knows it teases.

   CHORUS
   Wow! wow! wow!

I speak severely to my boy,
   I beat him when he sneezes;
For he can thoroughly enjoy
   The pepper when he pleases!

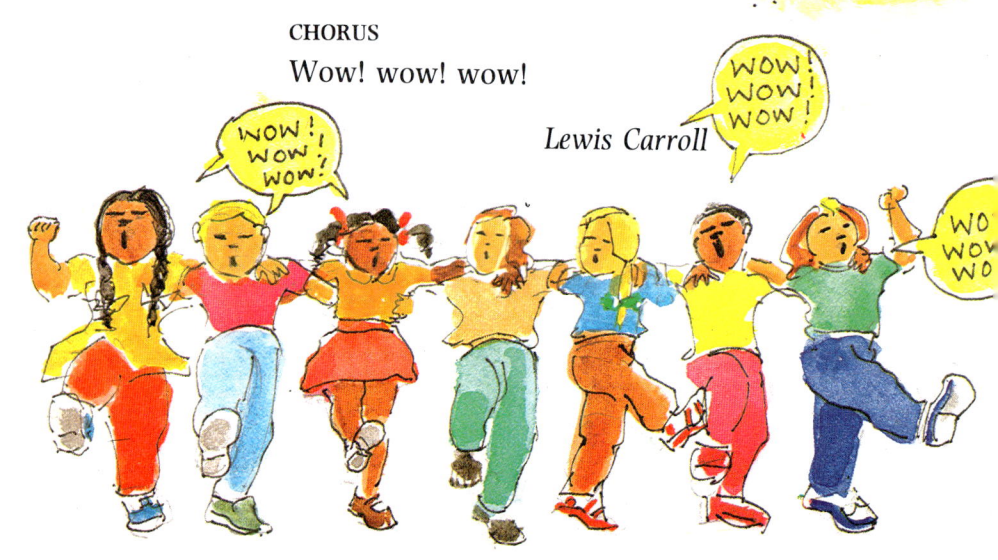

   CHORUS
   Wow! wow! wow!

Lewis Carroll

Pussy Cat, Pussy Cat

Pussy Cat, Pussy Cat

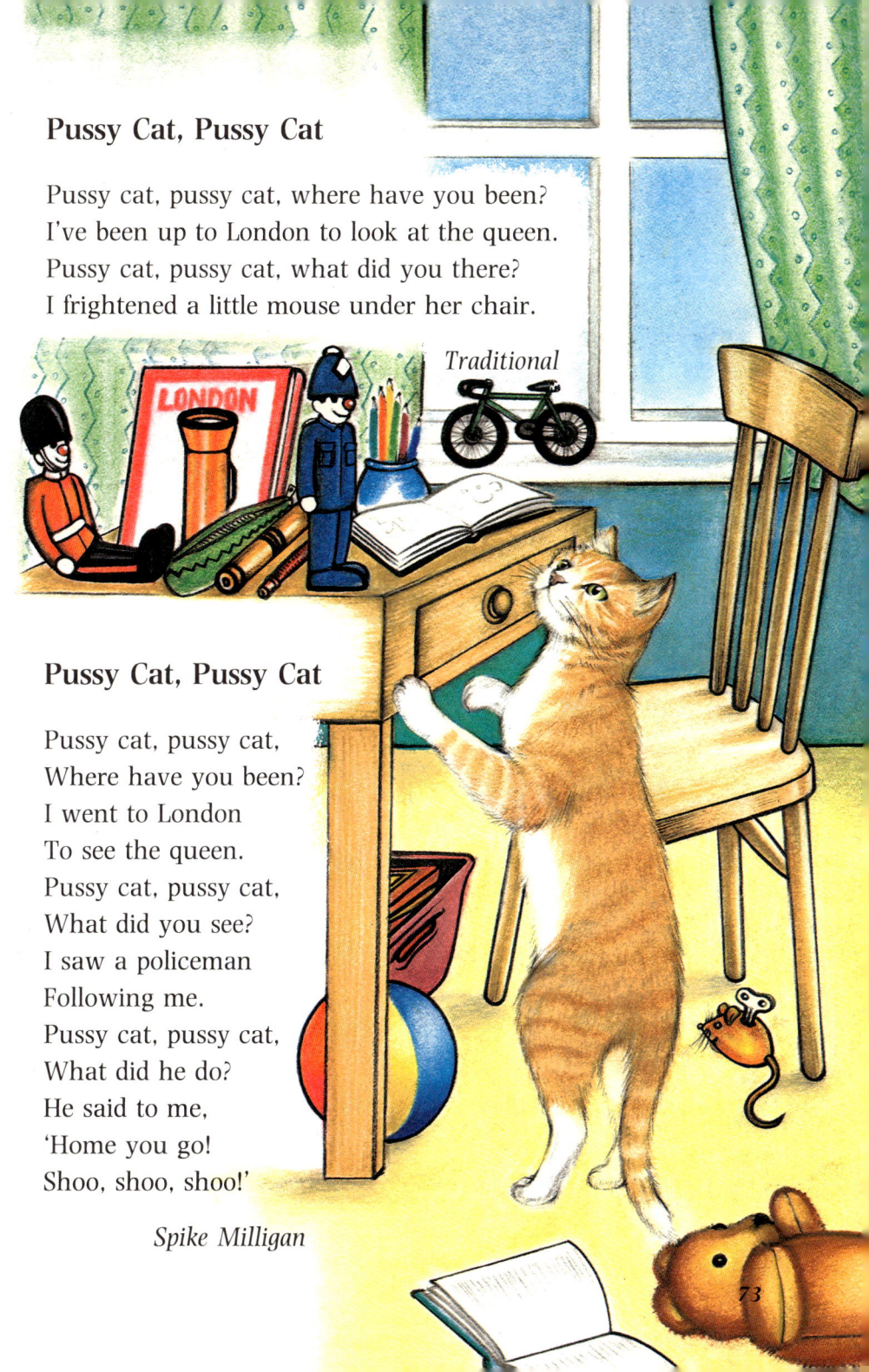

Pussy cat, pussy cat, where have you been?
I've been up to London to look at the queen.
Pussy cat, pussy cat, what did you there?
I frightened a little mouse under her chair.

Traditional

Pussy Cat, Pussy Cat

Pussy cat, pussy cat,
Where have you been?
I went to London
To see the queen.
Pussy cat, pussy cat,
What did you see?
I saw a policeman
Following me.
Pussy cat, pussy cat,
What did he do?
He said to me,
'Home you go!
Shoo, shoo, shoo!'

Spike Milligan

Fluffy

Tit for tat,
Catch a rat.

I have soft paws,
I purr and mew
I have sharp claws,
But not for you.

Tit for tat,
Catch a rat.

Edwin Thumboo

Who am I?

I am a cat
purring
in my sleeping box
in the kitchen.

I am a cat
scratching
at the table
sharpening my claws.

I am a cat
eating
nine lives gourmet.

Ian (aged 7)

If You . . .

If you,
Like me,
Were made of fur
And sun warmed you,
Like me,
You'd purr.

Karla Kuskin

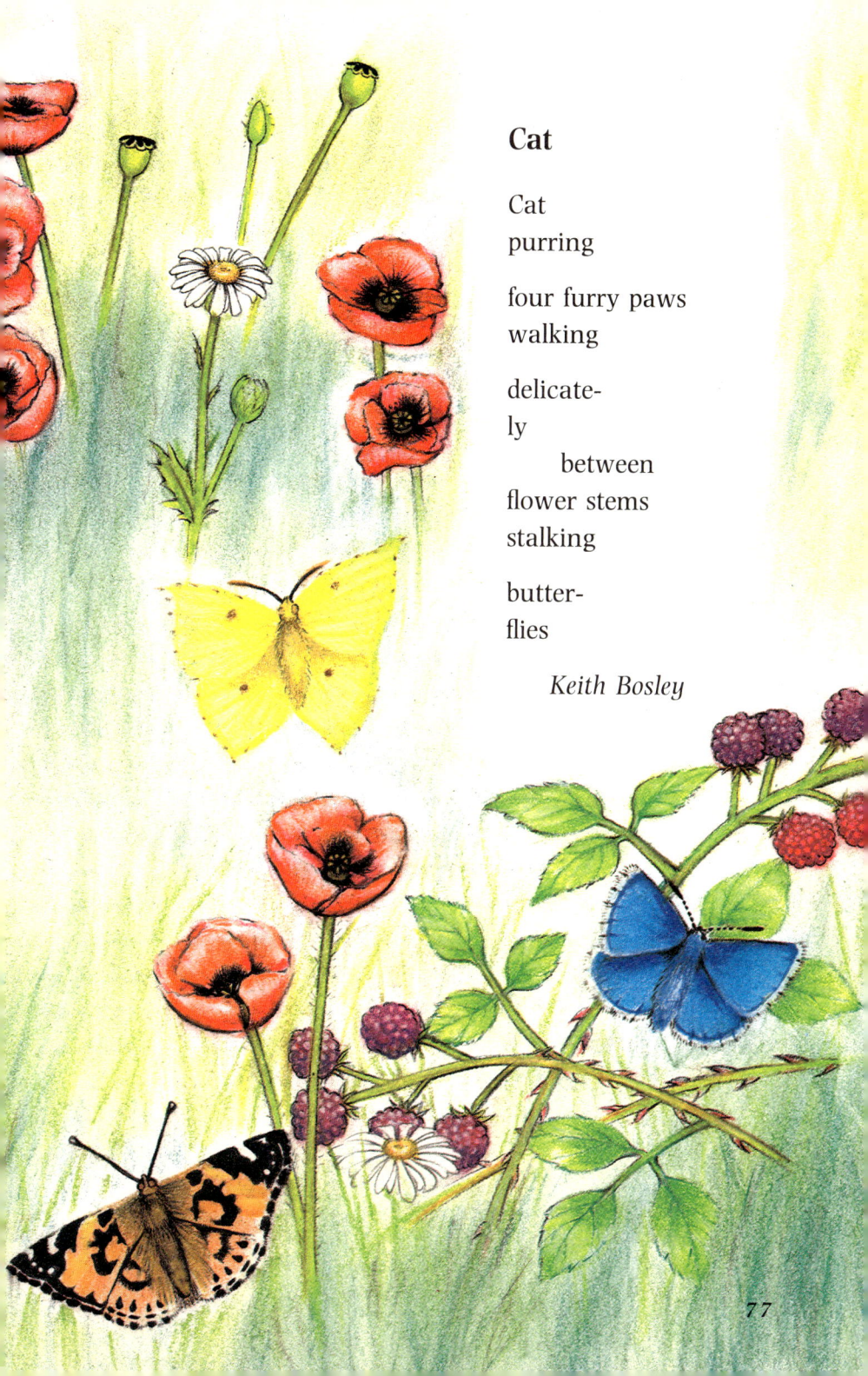

Cat

Cat
purring

four furry paws
walking

delicate-
ly
    between
flower stems
stalking

butter-
flies

Keith Bosley

Poem

As the cat
climbed over
the top of

the jamcloset
first the right
forefoot

carefully
then the hind
stepped down

into the pit of
the empty
flowerpot

William Carlos Williams

Why Did You Go?

why did you go
little four paws?
you forgot to shut
your big eyes.

where did you go?
like little kittens
are all the leaves
which open in the rain

little kittens who
are called spring,
is what we stroke
maybe asleep.

do you know? or maybe did
something go away
ever so quietly
when we weren't looking

e e cummings

A Kitten

He's nothing much but fur
And two round eyes of blue,
He has a giant purr
And a midget mew.

He darts and pats the air,
He starts and pricks his ear,
When there is nothing there
For him to see and hear.

He runs around in rings,
But why we cannot tell;
With sideways leaps he springs
At things invisible –

Then half-way through a leap
His startled eyeballs close,
And he drops off to sleep
With one paw on his nose.

Eleanor Farjeon

Cat

The spotted cat hops
Up to a white radiator-cover
As warm as summer, and there,

Between pots of green leaves growing,
By a window of cold panes showing
Silver of snow thin across the grass,

She settles slight neat muscles
Smoothly down within
Her comfortable fur,

Slips in the ends, front paws,
Tail, until she is readied,
Arranged, shaped for sleep.

Valerie Worth

The Cat

Creeping by night,
Creeping by night,
Creeping by night,
   Quoth the grey cat;
Creeping by night,
With neither star nor gleam,
Nor brightness nor light,
   Quoth the grey cat!

Traditional, Gaelic

On a Night of Snow

Cat, if you go out-doors you must walk in the snow,
You will come back with little white shoes on your feet,
Little white slippers of snow that have heels of sleet.
Stay by the fire, my Cat. Lie still, do not go.
See how the flames are leaping and hissing low,
I will bring you a saucer of milk like a marguerite,
So white and so smooth, so spherical and so sweet –
Stay with me, Cat. Out-doors the wild winds blow.

Out-doors the wild winds blow, Mistress, and dark is the night.
Strange voices cry in the trees, intoning strange lore
And more than cats move, lit by our eyes' green light,
On silent feet where the meadow grasses hang hoar –
Mistress, there are portents abroad of magic and might,
And things that are yet to be done. Open the door!

Elizabeth Coatsworth

85

EXTRACT FROM
Hunting with Henry the Cat

Small black-and-white cat –
white face white tummy white paws
sharp eyes sharp ears and
. . . very sharp claws

stretches out along the floor
scratches round his bowl, then

out of the door to the garden.

(But don't be fooled by his
slow and sleepy, easy walk – he's going
             hunting!)

A sunny path,
         he's lying with his front feet in
                  the air.
(He's very, very still,
he's *not* asleep . . .)

SNAP!

He's missed . . . a butterfly

Two wings of creamy-white
like fluttering crisps

(A snack that got away –
to flutter back another day?)

Rolls over, up and
prowling now – a Tiger in a Forest of
Chrysanthemums . . .

he's *hunting* – yes, but *what*?
        Caterpillars? . . . Centipedes?

(Anything That Moves, says Henry.)

Mick Gowar

Granny Tom

There's a cat among the pigeons
In the yard, in the yard,
And it seems he isn't trying
Very hard.
Should a pigeon chance to swoop,
You can see his whiskers droop
And his tail not twitch its loop
In the yard.

For the cat is growing old
In the yard, in the yard,
And the pigeons leave him cold.
He has starred
In his youth in many chases,
When he put them through their paces.
Now he knows just what his place is
In the yard.

He's a snoozer in the sun
And his hunting days are done.
He's a dozer by the wall
And he pounces not at all
For he knows he no more can. He
Might well be the pigeons' *granny*
In the yard!

Kit Wright

Fat Cat

I have such a fat
cat.
A greedy cat.
A lazy cat.

When bees are busy
and hot sun
shines
fat cat sleeps.

Lazy cat yawns.
Comes downstairs.
Mews
for her tea.

Greedy cat's belly,
full.
She sits in the garden's
shadow.
Watches martins
make circles
in the sky.

Yellow moon rises.
First star
Shines.
She's a wide-awake cat.
Not-so-fat-cat.
Gone for the night cat.
Goodbye.

Ann Bonner

Bring Back the Cat

Bring back the cat
Bring back the cat
My little girl say
Bring back the cat

Bring back the cat
Bring back the cat
My little girl
She really like that

My little girl she four in May
Got a pet kitten, it black and grey
Playing in the garden just the other day
Kitten went missing, must have gone astray
(Unless some kittennapper took her away)

Went right down to the RSPCA
Told me not to worry, it would be OK
Nothing more to do 'cept hope and pray
Maybe he bring it back some day
That why my little girl she say:

Bring back the cat
Bring back the cat
My little girl say
Bring back the cat

Bring back the cat
Bring back the cat
My little girl she
Really like that

Roger McGough

91

The Singing Cat

It was a little captive cat
Up in a crowded train
His mistress takes him from his box
To ease his fretful pain.

She holds him tight upon her knee
The graceful animal
And all the people look at him
He is so beautiful.

But oh he pricks and oh he prods
And turns upon her knee
Then lifteth up his innocent voice
In plaintive melody.

He lifteth up his innocent voice
He lifteth up, he singeth
And to each human countenance
A smile of grace he bringeth.

He lifteth up his innocent paw
Upon her breast he clingeth
And everybody cries, Behold
The cat, the cat that singeth.

He lifteth up his innocent voice
He lifteth up, he singeth
And all the people warm themselves
In the love his beauty bringeth.

Stevie Smith

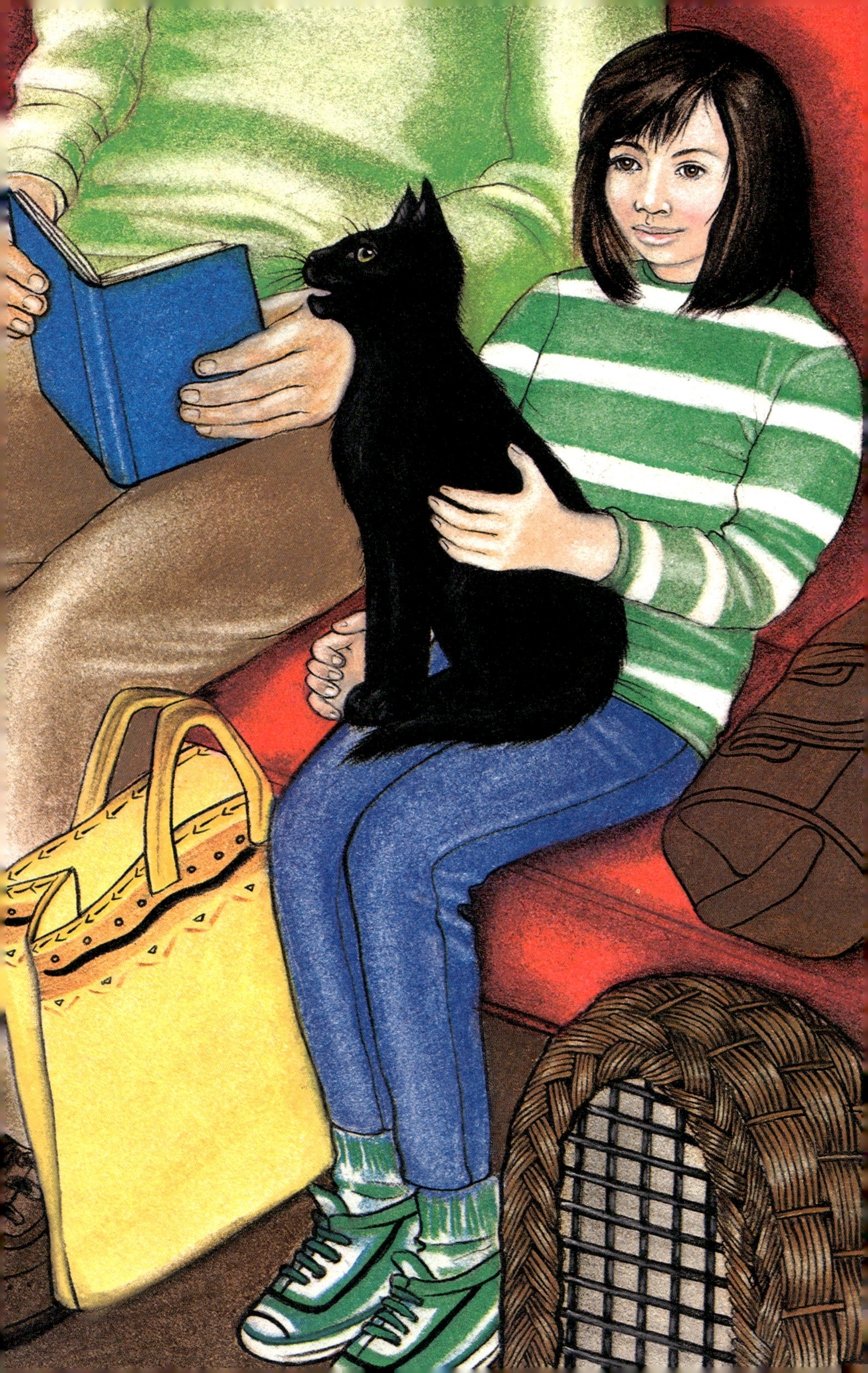

Uncle Paul of Pimlico

My Uncle Paul of Pimlico
Has seven cats as white as snow,
Who sit at his enormous feet
And watch him, as a special treat,
Play the piano upside down,
In his delightful dressing gown;
The firelight leaps, the parlour glows,
And, while the music ebbs and flows,
They smile (while purring the refrains),
At little thoughts that cross their brains.

Mervyn Peake

The Greater Cats

The greater cats with golden eyes
Stare out between the bars.
Deserts are there, and different skies,
And night with different stars.

Vita Sackville-West

Tiger

The tiger
Has swallowed
A black sun,

In his cold
Cage he
Carries it still:

Black flames
Flicker through
His fur,

Black rays soar
From the centres
Of his eyes.

Valerie Worth

EXTRACT FROM **India**

They hunt, the velvet tigers in the jungle,
The spotted jungle full of shapeless patches –
Sometimes they're leaves, sometimes they're hanging flowers,
Sometimes they're hot gold patches of the sun:
They hunt, the velvet tigers in the jungle!

W J Turner

There are Times

There are times when even
the tiger sleeps.

Chinese proverb

Roar

This is a tiger
Striped with black
You snarl at him
And he'll snarl back

SSNNAAARRRLLL

Karla Kuskin

Tiger, Tiger

Tiger, tiger, you scare me
With your coat soft and fair.
I do not dare
Go too near.

But when you are in a cage
I don't care.

You have sharp eyes,
Not like mine,
And sharp nails,
I bite mine.
Worst of all
Those big white teeth
Could eat me in one huge bite.

Sarah Harris (aged 8)

EXTRACT FROM The Tyger

Tyger Tyger, burning bright,
In the forests of the night;
What immortal hand or eye,
Could frame thy fearful symmetry?

William Blake

Acknowledgements

'Bananas in Pyjamas' reproduced by permission of Carey Blyton, composer/author; 'Jim-Jam Pyjamas' from *Jim-Jam Pyjamas* by Gina Wilson, Jonathan Cape, 1990; 'Ode to the Queen on her Jubilee' from *Startling Verse for All the Family* by Spike Milligan (Puffin Books), © Spike Milligan Productions; 'Humpty Dumpty' and 'This Little Pig' from *Hairy Tales and Nursery Crimes* by Michael Rosen, André Deutsch Ltd, 1986; 'Dis Lickle Pig' from *Jamaica Maddah Goose*, compiled by Donald Robertson, edited by Louise Bennett, reprinted with the permission of The Association of Friends of The Edna Manley For The Visual Arts (formerly The Jamaica School of Art); 'Back Yard, July Night' © 1969 by William Cole; 'Pet Food' by Terry Jones, reprinted by permission of Pavilion Books from *The Curse of the Vampire's Socks* by Terry Jones; 'Nature Poem' from *Nothingmas Day* by Adrian Mitchell, Allison & Busby, 1984, reprinted by permission of the author; 'The One who does not Love Me' by Ulli Beier from *Yoruba Poetry*, Cambridge University Press; 'Black Dot' copyright © Libby Houston 1973, 1987, originally commissioned and published by BBC Schools Radio for the programme *Stories and Rhymes*; 'P's and Q's' from *Nailing the Shadow* by Roger McGough (Viking Kestrel, 1987) and 'To Amuse Emus' from *An Imaginary Menagerie* by Roger McGough (Viking Kestrel), reprinted by permission of the Peters Fraser & Dunlop Group Ltd; 'Ruthless Rhyme Five' by Harry Graham from *Most Ruthless Rhymes for Heartless Homes*, Edward Arnold; 'Short Sharp Shock' is taken from *There's an Awful Lot of Weirdos in our Neighbourhood* © 1987 Colin McNaughton, first published in the UK by Walker Books Ltd; 'The Gentle Giant' by Dennis Lee, from *Jelly Belly*, published by Macmillan of Canada, © Dennis Lee; 'Have You Seen the Hidebehind' by Michael Rosen from *Mind Your Own Business*, André Deutsch, 1974; 'Dragon Night' by Jane Yolen, reprinted by permission of Curtis Brown Ltd. Copyright © 1980 by Jane Yolen; 'Sweet Dreams' reprinted by permission of Curtis Brown Ltd, copyright © 1961 by Ogden Nash.

'Kids' from *Startling Verse for All the Family* by Spike Milligan, copyright © Spike Milligan Productions; 'Don't' from *Don't Put Mustard in the Custard* by Michael Rosen, André Deutsch 1986; 'I Woke Up This Morning' from *Dogs and Dragons, Trees and Dreams* by Karla Kuskin. Originally published in *The Rose on My Cake* by Karla Kuskin. Copyright © 1964 by Karla Kuskin; 'Suzanna Socked Me Sunday' from *The New Kid on the Block* by Jack Prelutsky. William Heinemann Ltd 1986 and William Morrow & Co Inc; 'Bossy Parrot' © Emma Reid; 'Parents Never Understand' from *Spin a Soft Black Song* by Nikki Giovanni. Copyright © 1971, 1985 by Nikki Giovanni, reprinted by permission of Farrar, Straus & Giroux, Inc.; 'Monday's Child' from *There's an Awful Lot of Weirdos in Our Neighbourhood*, copyright © 1987 Colin McNaughton, first published in the UK by Walker Books Ltd; 'A-So it Go' by kind permission of John Agard c/o Caroline Sheldon Literary Agency, from *Laughter is an Egg* published by Viking Kestrel 1989; 'Dave Dirt Came to Dinner' by Kit Wright, from *Hot Dog and Other Poems* by Kit Wright (Kestrel, 1981), copyright © Kit Wright, 1981; Errol Lloyd for 'Blame the Parents'; 'Teacher Said . . .' reprinted by permission of Faber & Faber Ltd, from *Magic Mirror* by Judith Nicholls; 'Twiddling Your Thumbs' reprinted by permission of Faber & Faber Ltd from *Twiddling Your Thumbs* by Wendy Cope; 'Don't Call Alligator Longmouth Till You Cross River' from *Say it Again, Granny* by John Agard. The Bodley Head 1986; 'Good Morning, Mr Croco-doco-dile' from *Early in the Morning* by Charles Causley, Viking Kestrel 1986; 'Come Out With Me' from *Now We Are Six* by A A Milne. Copyright © 1927 by E.P. Dutton, renewed 1955 by A A Milne. Reprinted by permission of the publisher, Dutton Children's Books, a division of Penguin Books USA Inc., and Methuen Children's Books; 'Father and I in the Woods' from *One at a Time* by David McCord. Copyright 1952 by David McCord. By permission of Harrap & Co and Little, Brown & Co; an extract from 'Clearances' reprinted by permission of Faber & Faber Ltd from *The Haw Lantern* by Seamus Heaney; 'Rules' by Brian Patten, from *Gargling with Jelly* by Brian Patten (Kestrel, 1985), copyright © Brian Patten, 1985.

'Pussy Cat, Pussy Cat' by Spike Milligan from *Startling Verse for All the Family*, Puffin Books, © Spike Milligan Productions; 'Fluffy' by Edwin Thumboo from *Child's Delight*, Federal Publishers Singapore, 1972 © Edwin Thumboo; 'If You, Like Me . . .' from *Dogs and Dragons, Trees and Dreams* by Karla Kuskin. 'If You, Like Me' originally appeared in *Any Me I Want to Be* by Karla Kuskin. Copyright © 1972 by Karla Kuskin; 'Cat' from *And I Dance* by Keith Bosley, reproduced by kind permission of Angus & Robertson Publishers; 'Poem' from *Collected Poems of William Carlos Williams, 1909-1939, vol I*, copyright 1938 by New Directions Publishing Corp., reprinted by permission of New Directions Publishing Corp and Carcanet Press Ltd; 'Why Did You Go?' from *Complete Poems 1913-1962* by E. E. Cummings, reprinted by permission of Granada Books, part of HarperCollins Publishers – 'Why Did You Go' is also reprinted from *Tulips and Chimneys* by E. E. Cummings, edited by George James Firmage, by permission of Liveright Publishing Corporation. Copyright 1923, 1925 and renewed 1951, 1953 by E. E. Cummings. Copyright © 1973, 1976 by the Trustees for the E. E. Cummings Trust. Copyright © 1973, 1976 by George James Firmage; 'A Kitten' by Eleanor Farjeon from *Invitation to a Mouse*, Hodder and Stoughton 1986; 'Cat' from *Small Poems* by Valerie Worth, poems copyright © 1972 by Valerie Worth, reprinted by permission of Farrar, Straus & Giroux, Inc; 'On a Night of Snow' by Elizabeth Coatsworth from *Night and the Cat*, Macmillan Publishing Co. by permission of Margaret Beston; extract from 'Hunting with Henry the Cat' by Mick Gowar, from *Third Time Lucky* by Mick Gowar (Viking Kestrel, 1988) copyright © Mick Gowar, 1988; 'Granny Tom' by Kit Wright, from *Cat Among the Pigeons* by Kit Wright (Viking Kestrel, 1988), copyright © Kit Wright, 1988; 'Fat Cat' by Ann Bonner by permission of the author; 'Bring Back the Cat' by Roger McGough, reprinted by permission of the Peters Fraser & Dunlop Group Ltd; 'The Singing Cat' by Stevie Smith from *Collected Poems*, Penguin Books Ltd, by permission of James MacGibbon; 'Uncle Paul of Pimlico' by Mervyn Peake from *Rhymes Without Reason*, Methuen Children's Books, © 1974 Maeve Peake; 'The Greater Cats' by Vita Sackville-West © Nigel Nicolson; 'Tiger' from *Small Poems Again* by Valerie Worth, poems copyright © 1975, 1986 by Valerie Worth, reprinted by permission of Farrar, Straus & Giroux, Inc; extract from 'India' from *Selected Poems of W J Turner*, Oxford University Press, 1939; 'There are Times' from *700 Chinese Proverbs*, collected and translated by Henry Hart, © Stanford University Press; 'Roar' by Karla Kuskin from *Roar and More*. Copyright © 1956 by Karla Kuskin.

Every effort has been made to reach copyright holders; the publishers would be glad to hear from anyone whose rights they have unknowingly infringed.

Index of first lines

a black dot/a jelly tot   28
As your bright and tiny spark   19
Ask no questions   51
As the cat/climbed over   78
Bananas,/In pyjamas,   9
Bring back the cat   90
Call alligator long-mouth   60
Cat, if you go outdoors you must walk in the snow,   84
Cat/purring   77
Creeping by night,   83
Dave Dirt came to dinner   53
Dis lickle pig go a markit,   14
Don't do,/Don't do,   42
Every night/At twelve o'clock   32
Father heard his children scream,   31
Firefly, airplane, satellite, star –   19
Get set, ready now, jump right in   24
Good morning, Mr Croco-doco-dile,   61
Governments rule most countries,   66
Have you seen the Hidebehind?   34
Here am I,/Little Jumping Joan;   26
He's nothing much but fur   80
He wears striped jim-jam pyjamas   10
Humpty Dumpty sat on a wall,   12
I am a cat   75
I blame the parents   54
If you,/Like me   76
If your children are ever unruly,   31
I have such a fat/cat,   89
I quite often confuse   30
It was a little captive cat   92
I woke up this morning   44
I wonder as into bed I creep   36
Little flame mouths,   35
Monday's child is red and spotty,   49
Mother made a seedy cake,   59
Mummy says never run on the road,   58
Mum said, PIANO! Emma,   47
My Uncle Paul of Pimlico   94
Pardon me/for being so rude   59
Piggy on the railway   13

103

Policeman, policeman/don't catch me!   52
Polished linoleum shone there. Brass taps shone,   64
Pussy cat, pussy cat where have you been?   73
'Sit up straight,'/Said Mum to Mabel   41
Skylark, what prompts your silver song   22
Small black-and-white cat –   86
So mouthy-mouthy/so mouthy-mouthy   50
'Son,'/My father used to say,   63
Sound the trumpet,/Bang the drum   11
Speak roughly to your little boy   68
Suzanna socked me Sunday,   46
The greater cats with golden eyes   95
The man in the wilderness asked of me,   16
The one who does not love me,   27
There are times when even/the tiger sleeps,   97
There's a cat among the pigeons   88
There's sun on the river and sun on the hill . . .   62
There was an old man in a tree,   17
This little pig went to market,   15
The spotted cat hops/Up to a white radiator-cover   82
The tiger/Has swallowed   96
The winds they did blow,   23
They hunt, the velvet tigers in the jungle,   97
This is a tiger   98
Tiger, tiger, you scare me   99
Tit for tat,/Catch a rat,   74
To amuse/emus   30
Twinkle, twinkle little bat!   18
Tyger Tyger, burning bright   100
well i can't 'cause/yesterday when mommy had   48
What a wonderful bird the frog are –   29
What do you get, Jude,   20
When you've finished all your writing   56
why did you go/little four paws?   79
You can use/mumbled and muttered,   55